The you&me

WORKBOOK

A Book That Teaches Social Skills and Social Awareness

By
Lisa M. Schab

Childswork
ChildsPLAY

CALL 1·800·962·1141

The You & Me Workbook
A Book That Teaches Social Skills and Social Awareness

By Lisa M. Schab

Childswork/Childsplay publishes products for mental health professionals, teachers and parents who wish to help children with their developmental, social and emotional growth. For questions, comments, or to request a free catalog describing hundreds of games, toys, books, and other counseling tools, call 1-800-962-1141.

© 2001 Childswork/Childsplay, LLC
A Guidance Channel Company
PO Box 760
Plainview, NY 11803
1-800-962-1141

ISBN 1-58815-037-2

Table of Contents

Table of Contents

Introduction for Adults

Getting along is easy for some people, while it is very difficult for others. No one masters the skill perfectly. However, social skills can be learned. The mere condition of being alive affords us the daily opportunity to acquire social skills.

An infant begins to learn social skills the minute he is born. Although his ability to reason is extremely limited, he can see and hear the people sharing his world. He hears polite and harsh words; he sees kind and cruel conduct. He observes people interacting with each other and witnesses the consequences of many types of behavior. He learns social skills through "modeling."

An infant also learns through "direct teaching." Her parents instruct her to say "Please," "Thank you," "Hello," and "Good-bye." She is reprimanded when she is rude to adults and praised when she gets along with her siblings. If she lives in an emotionally healthy family, she learns appropriate methods to communicate, express feelings, and manage conflict.

Not all children, however, acquire adequate social skills. Some may be overly shy while others are overly aggressive; some may hesitate to form relationships in an effort to avoid conflict or confrontation; others may delve into dependent relationships, attributable to an underlying fear of being hurt or abandoned.

When children are formally taught the basic skills necessary to begin and sustain healthy relationships, they may feel more confident in pursuing connections with other people. The exercises in this workbook are designed to teach fundamental social skills and are divided into six main areas of content.

1. Meeting New People: This section teaches where and what to look for in potential friends, how to approach people and start conversations, and specific behaviors and words that may increase or decrease the chance of being accepted by others.

2. Talking with People: This section teaches techniques to begin and sustain conversations, the benefits of balanced communication, and the importance of listening.

3. Understanding People: This section teaches feelings identification in oneself and others, how to see life from another person's point of view, and how to make educated and caring choices about actions toward other people.

4. When People Hurt Us: This section teaches self-confidence, effective ways to respond to teasing and bullying, behaviors that may diminish teasing and bullying, and personal safety.

5. Solving Problems with People: This section teaches responsibility for one's own actions, specific problem-solving steps, and behaviors that tend to increase or decrease interpersonal problems.

6. Managing Conflict with People: This section teaches healthy ways to communicate feelings, express anger, and manage and resolve conflicts.

By discussing the information presented and completing the activities in each area, a child can learn and practice basic concepts of social interaction. The most effective learning takes place when the child is guided through the exercises by an adult and provided the opportunity to practice specific skills repeatedly until they are mastered.

Permission is granted to duplicate these activity pages for personal and professional use. Some exercises require scissors, glue, tape, pencils, pens, crayons and markers.

When attempting to increase children's social skills, the introduction of some very practical concepts is the first step.

Children can learn what environments are most conducive to making friends, what characteristics to look for in potential friends, and how to approach new people to initiate conversations.

Children can also learn specific behaviors and words that will increase their chance of being accepted by others.

While introducing oneself and starting conversations may seem routine and simple to some, many children experience anxiety in these situations. However, these children can gain confidence, and possibly reduce their anxiety levels, by learning and practicing specific actions when meeting new people.

Activity: Who Will Be My Friend?

Objective: **To understand there is a better chance of making friends with people with whom I have something in common and to practice recognizing these people.**

. . . .

It is easier to make friends with people when we have personal characteristics or interests in common.

Help Jenny make friends by writing what she has in common with each of the people pictured below. When you are done, draw a star by the people with whom she has the most in common.

Activity: Putting on a Friendly Face

Objective: To understand that a smile sends a friendly message to others.

• •

   What we show on our face often tells other people what kind of a mood we are in. A smiling face tells others we are feeling friendly and eager to meet them.

   Draw a picture of what you look like when you are wearing a friendly smile.

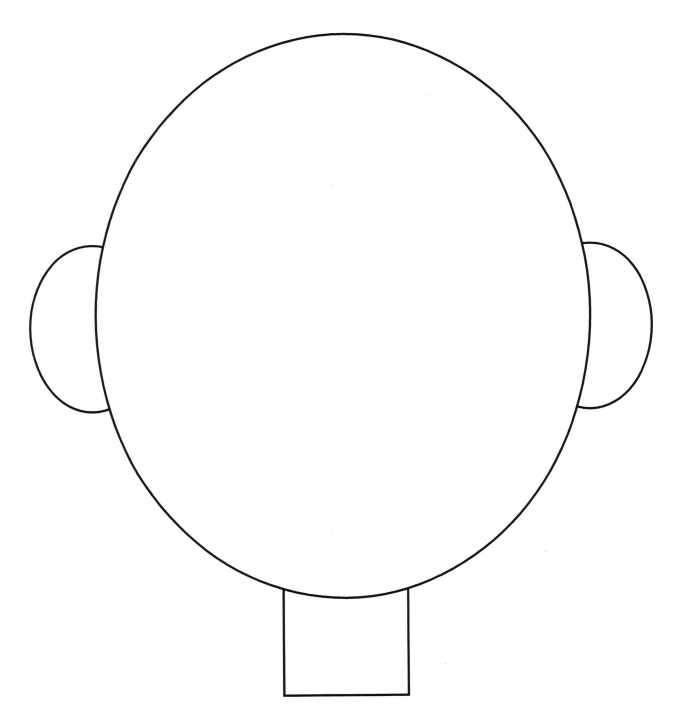

9

Area 1: Meeting New People

Activity: It's What's Inside That Counts

Objective: To understand that inner qualities are more important than looks or material possessions when choosing a friend.

. . . .

When choosing friends it is important to find out what people are like on the inside. This is more important than what they look like or how much they own. The people who make the best friends are those who have good inner qualities and who treat you well.

You can learn something about each of the people below by looking at them on the outside. To find out what they are like on the inside, hold this page up to a mirror. Then color the pictures of those people who have the inner qualities that would make them good friends.

Area 1: Meeting New People

Activity: First Words

Objective: To identify friendly greetings.

. . . .

A friendly greeting tells people that you are open to making new friends. It is a good idea to have a few friendly greetings ready, so that you have something to say when you meet someone for the first time.

Find and circle the friendly greetings (HI, HELLO, WHAT'S UP, HEY, GOOD MORNING, HOW DO YOU DO) in the Word Search below.

```
G Y T Z V B K C P L B
K O J M R H F Q H P H
R N O K T O Y Z I L E
H V T D D W R K A P L
L W N C M D D V P J L
K W D F Z O T M R R O
B J K W C Y R G B D S
S L M G D U R N T O B
Y L D Y F D C Z I L D
E F W S M O P D Y N C
H R C P U S T A H W G
```

Activity: What Should I Say?

Objective: To practice using appropriate words when meeting people.

• •

Sometimes we know the right words to say when meeting new people, but we find it hard to say them. Practicing in advance can make it easier.

The people below are meeting for the first time, and they want to be friendly. What do you think they could say to each other? Write the friendly greetings they might use in the conversation balloons by their heads. Then practice saying them to someone else who is willing to role-play with you.

Area 1: Meeting New People

Activity: Introductions

Objective: To learn how to make an introduction.

When you meet others for the first time, it is polite to tell them your name. Listen to what their names are, too. Then you can use their names later in the conversation. When you address others by name, it tells them you are interested in them.

Name the creatures below so they can introduce themselves. Put in your own name, too!

Activity: Comments and Compliments

Objective: To use comments and compliments to start conversations.

••

Offering friendly comments and giving sincere compliments are two ways to start conversations with other people. A comment is a statement about something that you notice, such as, "It sure is cold today" or "I like this kind of pizza." A compliment is a positive statement about another person, such as, "I like your hair" or "Wow, you are a good soccer player!"

Practice thinking of and giving comments and compliments by playing the following game, either alone or with someone else. Color the heart, star, flower and bird and cut them out. These are the game pawns. Flip a coin to determine how many spaces to move. If the coin lands on "heads," move one space. If the coin lands on "tails," move two spaces. When a player reaches FINISH, the game is over. Every player who has learned one new way to start a conversation is a winner.

START

FINISH

15

Activity: The Five W's

Objective: To ask questions to start conversations.

• •

Asking friendly questions is another way to start conversations. If you remember "The Five W's," you will always have a question to ask. "The Five W's" are who, what, when, where and why.

To practice asking questions, pretend you are a newspaper reporter who must write a story about each of the four pictures below. It is your job to gather all the facts for the story. Write a who, what, when, where and why question about each of these pictures.

Who? _____

What? _____

When? _____

Where? _____

Why? _____

Who? _____

What? _____

When? _____

Where? _____

Why? _____

Who? _____

What? _____

When? _____

Where? _____

Why? _____

Who? _____

What? _____

When? _____

Where? _____

Why? _____

Area 1: Meeting New People

Activity: Garden of Friends

Objective: To identify the characteristics of friendly/safe and unfriendly/unsafe peer groups.

• •

If you would like to join a new group of kids, watch them for a while to make sure they are behaving in friendly and safe ways. Groups who behave in friendly and safe ways are more likely to treat you kindly and want to be friends with you. Joining groups whose members are acting in unsafe and unfriendly ways may get you into trouble.

Practice identifying friendly/safe and unfriendly/unsafe actions by planting your own Garden of Friends. Read the words on the flower stems. If the stem describes a friendly or safe characteristic, draw a flower on the top of the stem. If the stem describes an unfriendly or unsafe characteristic, draw thorns on the stem. Color the flowers that are friendly and glue or tape them into your Garden of Friends on the next page.

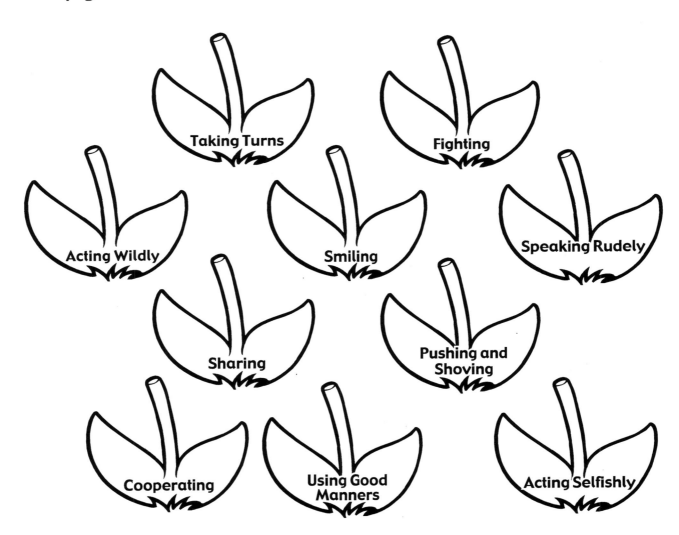

Activity: Search for a Friend

Objective: To identify people who might be open to having a new friend.

· ·

Some people are more open and willing to make new friends than others. Most of the time their willingness has little or nothing to do with you. It often depends upon what kind of mood they are in, what they are doing at the moment, and what kind of personality they have.

Color the faces of the children who look like they would most likely be open to meeting a new friend. Tell someone your reasons for choosing these children.

Whether shy or outgoing, all children can benefit from learning some basic principles of appropriate conversation. Quiet children who have difficulty with self-expression can gain confidence by learning techniques to initiate and carry on conversations. Children who dominate conversations can learn the benefits of balanced communication and the importance of listening.

Good manners, a positive attitude, and showing interest in other people are skills that can increase children's ability to communicate appropriately and effectively.

Once children feel confident about their ability to communicate, they naturally feel more comfortable with others.

Activity: Polite Words

Objective: **To learn words and phrases that demonstrate good manners.**

People who use good manners and speak politely to others make friends more easily than people who are rude and inconsiderate. Polite speech often includes three common words and phrases.   When you make a habit of using these polite words, you will find people usually respond to you in a friendly way.

These three words and phrases of polite speech are hidden in the picture below. To find out what they are, color the spaces as follows: stars, blue; dots, green; smiling faces, orange.

Activity: Good Manners

Objective: To practice good manners.

· ·

When people use polite words, others say they have good manners. People with good manners are usually well liked and get along with almost everyone they meet.

Practice using good manners by telling Petey the Polite Puppy which polite words (please, thank you, excuse me) to use in each of the situations described below.

_____

_____

22

Activity: Common Interests

Objective: To understand that common interests provide topics for conversation.

Sometimes people feel uncomfortable because they don't know what to say when they meet someone new. One place to start is by talking about anything that you have in common with the other person: likes, dislikes, interests, and personal characteristics.

In each of the frames below, draw a picture of someone you know or someone with whom you would like to become friends. Next to each picture, write three things you have in common with that person.

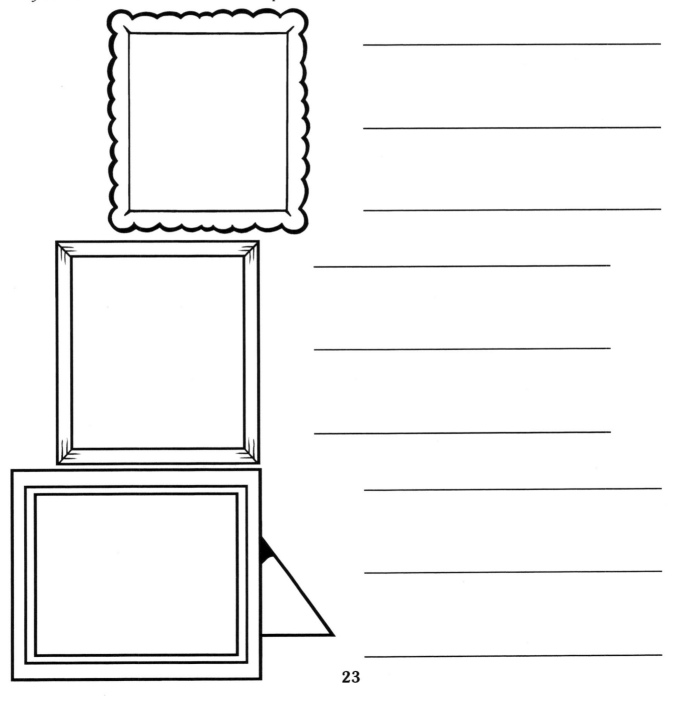

Activity: Conversation Train

Objective: To use questions to keep a conversation going.

Sometimes even people with a lot of things in common run out of topics to discuss. Asking a question can keep the conversation going and shows you are interested in the other person.

See how long you can make the following Conversation Train. Cut out the train cars and glue or tape them behind the train engine. Think of your own questions and write them in the empty cars. Use extra paper to make more cars if you like. The more questions you add to the Conversation Train, the longer it will be.

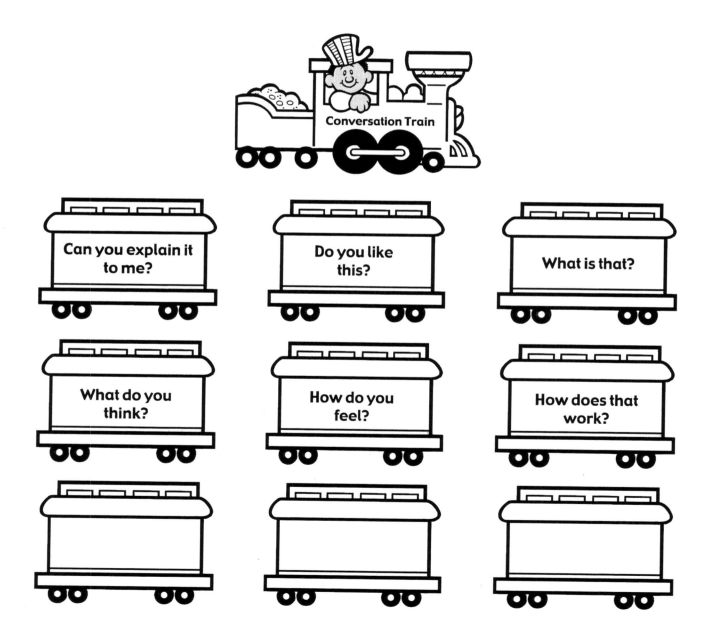

Conversation Train

Can you explain it to me?

Do you like this?

What is that?

What do you think?

How do you feel?

How does that work?

Activity: Two Ears, One Mouth

Objective: To learn that listening is an important social skill.

• •

Listening to others when they are speaking is a sign of respect and caring. However, sometimes it is hard to really pay attention to what others are saying. And, at other times, it is difficult not to interrupt others when they are talking.

When you look in the mirror, you see that you have two ears and only one mouth. Let this remind you that, when you are making friends, it is twice as important to listen as it is to talk.

Unscramble the words below, and draw a picture of the word in the frame above it. Does everyone have two ears and one mouth?   YES _____   NO _____

gpi	**mmo**	**tca**

_____   _____   _____

add	**kyenom**	**etchera**

_____   _____   _____

Area 2: Talking with People

Activity: A Winning Team

Objective: To learn listening behaviors.

• •

When you use good listening skills, other people feel you are interested in what they have to say. They will want to be with you more because they know you care about their feelings and opinions.

A good listener is one who exhibits the following behaviors:

- Makes eye contact with the speaker

- Doesn't interrupt

- Acknowledges she is listening by saying "Oh," "I see," and "Uh huh"

- Nods occasionally, indicating she understands what the speaker is saying

- Asks questions about what the speaker has said

Two teams are competing to win a social skills game. The team in the black uniform is winning because its members are using good listening skills. The team in the white uniform is losing because its members are using poor listening skills. Pretend you have been called in to coach the White Team. It is half time, and the team needs your help. On the chalkboard on the next page, write down some behavioral changes the White Team could make to become better listeners and score more points.

26

Half Time Advice

Activity: Something to Talk About

Objective: To practice the "give and take" of conversation.

• •

    A friendly two-party conversation is balanced: It goes back and forth between both participants. Both people have a chance to talk, and both people have a chance to listen. A conversation keeps moving when the first person speaks, followed by the second person making a comment or asking a question about what was said. Then the first person makes another comment or asks a question. Both participants take turns sharing information.

    Paul and Sandra have forgotten how to have a conversation. Can you help them? Cut out the subject pictures below and glue or tape one into the subject box at the top of the next page. This gives Paul and Sandra something to talk about. Next, get the conversation started by writing a comment or question about the subject in Paul's conversation balloon. Write an appropriate response, either a comment or question, in Sandra's conversation balloon. Keep the conversation going until all the conversation balloons have been filled. Then glue or tape another picture into the subject box. Continue until all the pictures have been discussed.

Subject Box

Activity: Stop the Complaining

Objective: To teach the value of a positive attitude and the difference between positive statements and complaints.

· ·

Everyone complains once in awhile, but no one likes to listen to someone who complains all the time. It is more fun to be with people who look on the positive side of things.

Help stop the complaining! Color the octagons red and cut them out. Then read the sentences on the next page and decide which are positive statements and which are complaints. Glue or tape the octagons over the complaints. Write the word STOP on the octagons to make them look like STOP signs.

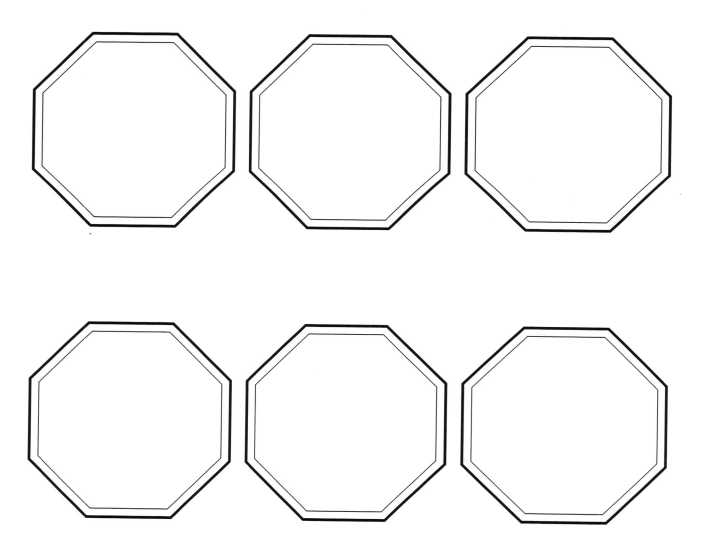

I feel good.

This ice cream tastes great.

I hate Mondays.

Skating is fun.

We never do things my way.

The game is so boring.

Even if it's raining, we can still have fun.

There's nothing to do at Grandma's house.

Exercising is a waste of time.

You are my best friend.

I like reading.

My brother is a brat.

Activity: The Positive Play

Objective: To learn how to give positive feedback.

• •

You can show friendliness toward other people by using positive statements when you speak with them. Giving positive feedback tells them you care about them and want to support them. Positive feedback encourages other people; and, when you give it, you feel good, too.

Read the statements listed below. Draw a line through the negative ones, and circle the positive ones. Then help the actors on the next page find lines for their Positive Play by writing the positive statements in the actors' empty conversation balloons.

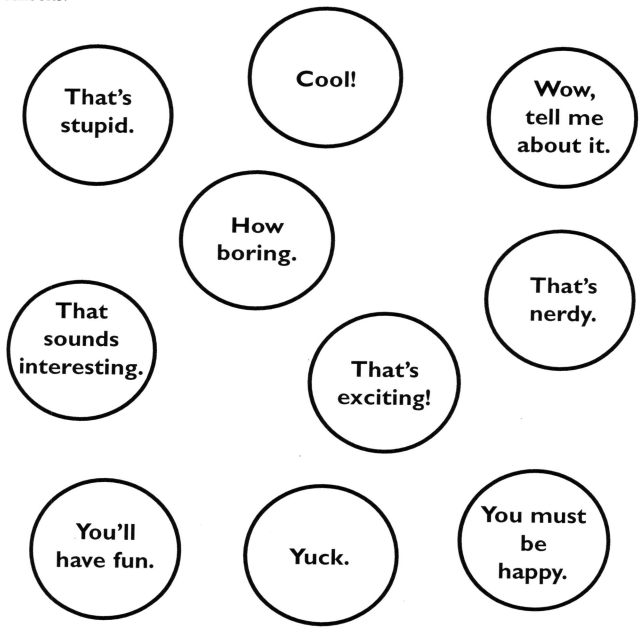

33

Activity: Showing Interest

Objective: To learn how to show interest in other people.

· ·

It is not always easy to convey the message that you are interested in other people. Sometimes you are worried about something or you have a lot to do and feel stressed. But if you practice and learn just a few skills now, you will be able to show interest in others at any time. When you are talking with someone in a friendly and polite manner, you are showing interest in what they are saying.

Read the words and phrases in each of the basketballs below. If you think that saying the statement in a particular basketball would "score you points" as a friendly person, draw a line from that basketball to the basketball hoop. If you think that saying the statement would "lose you points" as a friendly person, put an X over that basketball.

Personality is formed by a unique combination of genetics and life experiences. Because each human combination is different, we all experience a slightly, or greatly, different perception of life. While we may not always agree with another person's perception, understanding and accepting our differences can help us resolve problems.

The first step children need to take in order to understand and accept other people's feelings is to learn about their own. Then they are able to develop empathy, viewing life from another person's point of view and understanding how their words and actions affect others. Empathetic children can make educated and caring choices about the actions they take toward others.

Activity: Galaxy of Feelings

Objective: To identify a variety of feelings.

Human beings experience many feelings over the course of a lifetime, and even over the course of a day. The most common feelings are happy, sad, angry and scared. However, we experience many more feelings than these four.

Pretend you are an astronaut. You have been asked to travel to the Galaxy of Feelings and give names to all the stars. Your backpack is stuffed with feeling names. Choose one feeling name for each star below. Match the feelings to the expressions on the faces of the stars, and write in the feeling names on the lines provided.

Area 3: Understanding People

Activity: The Feelings Forest

Objective: To become aware of and identify my feelings.

• •

Sometimes we are so busy with school, friends, family and after-school activities, we don't take the time to know what we are feeling. When we are not in touch with our feelings, we may have a difficult time getting along with others. We need to ask ourselves the following question many times throughout the day: What am I feeling right now?

Take a walk through The Feelings Forest by drawing a line along the path. You will meet many different creatures in the forest who will describe situations that might have happened to you. If the situation did happen to you, tell the creature about it. In the space provided, write the name of your feeling (happy, sad, angry, scared, etc.) and describe how you felt at the time.

Activity: The Feelings Detective

Objective: To recognize signs of other people's feelings.

••

If you observe carefully, you can tell how people are feeling by the way their faces and bodies look. Once you know how they feel, you can decide the best way to act toward them.

Pretend you are The Feelings Detective. Look carefully at the pictures below to gather clues about what each child is feeling. Write the clues you find in the spaces next to their pictures. Write what you think they are feeling on the lines below their pictures.

_____   _____

_____   _____

_____   _____

_____   _____

_____   _____

_____   _____

_____   _____

_____   **39**   _____

Activity: Let's Pretend

Objective: To understand what it feels like to be someone else.

••

Since no one is exactly the same as anyone else, everyone sees life differently. The best way to understand another person's thoughts and feelings is to imagine what it might feel like to be that other person.

Each of the rings below belongs to a different person. Color and cut out each ring, bend it into a circle, and glue or tape the ends together. Put each ring on your finger, one at a time, and pretend to be the person whose ring you are wearing. Really think about how it would feel to be that person. Then write about it on the lines below.

firefighter_____

doctor_____

mother_____

pilot _____

Activity: Caring Words

Objective: To identify words that show caring.

• •

One of the best presents you can give someone is to say you care about her. No material gift can ever do what a show of concern does. Kind words are priceless gifts that are usually appreciated far more than anything that can be bought in a store.

Below is a picture of Susan who is feeling very sad. You want to give Susan gifts to make her feel better. Both caring and non-caring words and phrases are written in the gifts that surround her. Color those gifts that would show Susan you care about her.

Activity: Caring Gestures

Objective: To identify actions that show caring.

• •

People's actions show how they care about the people in their lives. Their actions can tell others if they are kind and loving or mean and thoughtless. Talking, listening, sharing, and smiling are ways others tell us they want to be our friend. Hugging us, holding our hand, and helping us when we need it are ways people show they care about us.

Look through a magazine for photographs of people showing that they care for one another. Cut them out and glue or tape them in The Caring Frame below.

The Caring Frame

Area 3: Understanding People

Activity: Favor Coupons

Objective: To think about and practice ways of caring for others.
••

There are hundreds of little things we can do to show others how we feel about them. Most of these don't cost a lot of money and don't take a lot of time. A little gesture of love, concern, affection or caring can make someone else happy for a whole day!

Think of all the people in your life whom you care about and love. You can show them how you feel by giving them a special present, a Favor Coupon. You might give your mom or dad a Favor Coupon good for a hug or one night of washing the dishes. You might give your friend a Favor Coupon for a candy bar or the first turn on your scooter on Saturday. Fill in the blank spaces on the Favor Coupons below. Then color and cut them out. If you would like to have more Favor Coupons to give away, photocopy the ones below before you fill them out.

To: _____

From: _____

Good for: _____

To: _____

From: _____

Good for: _____

To: _____

From: _____

Good for: _____

To: _____

From: _____

Good for: _____

Activity: Someone to Listen to Us

Objective: To teach the value of listening as a caring gesture.

Carefully listening to others is one of the best ways to show you care about them. It takes time and patience to really listen. Good listeners make great friends. People who develop listening skills almost always make a lot of friends, many of whom become lifelong pals.

Eddie the Elephant is a great listener. Pretend the situations below are happening to you. Whisper into Eddie's ear, telling him how you feel about each situation and what your thoughts are.

- **You got a new puppy.**
- **You failed a science test.**
- **You fell off the playground equipment and broke your arm.**

- **Your little brother lost all the pieces to your new game.**
- **You just got back from vacation.**
- **You scored the winning goal for your team.**

Activity: Time Alone

Objective: To understand that sometimes the best way to help people is to let them have some time alone.

. . . .

Sometimes when we are upset, it helps to talk with or to be with other people. But sometimes we just need a little time by ourselves to be quiet or to rest. Sometimes we don't want to have to talk to or to be with anyone else.

Amy is feeling sad because her favorite hamster just died. Everyone wants to help Amy feel better. Her friends ask her to come out and play. Her brother wants her to watch the goldfish with him. Her parents want to take her to the zoo. But Amy doesn't want to do any of these things. She just wants to be alone for a while. Color the pictures below. Then draw a line from Amy to the places she could go to be alone.

Activity: Act and Feel

Objective: To understand how my behavior affects others.

• •

Fill in the faces in the left column so they look like you. Pretend you have a friend named Billy, and you act toward him as described in the middle column. How does Billy feel when you do these things? Fill in Billy's expression on the faces in the right column to show how he feels when you act this way toward him.

1. You share your toys with Billy.

2. You break Billy's action figure.

3. You laugh at Billy when he falls off his bike.

4. You push Billy into the pool.

5. You help Billy study.

46

Every child is a target for being hurt by others. However, a child with high self-esteem is less likely to be teased or bullied. Feeling good about one's own worth, and acting on that feeling, makes a child more resistant to put-downs and intimidation.

Children can make themselves less vulnerable to teasing and bullying by the way they respond to them. Children can learn to eliminate behaviors that make them susceptible to taunting. A positive, kind and generous attitude will, most likely, elicit the same from other people.

There are times when teasing or bullying may become extreme, threatening a child's safety. At these times it is important for the child to understand that adult assistance is a necessary intervention.

Activity: Trophy Collection

Objective: To raise self-esteem by recognizing personal abilities.

• •

Everyone has a special talent or skill. Everyone is a "winner" at something. Maybe you are a good swimmer, a good reader, or a good singer. Maybe you make great peanut butter sandwiches or know how to make up scary stories. Maybe you are good at climbing trees or giving hugs.

You deserve recognition! Think of things you do well. Color the trophies below, and write something that you do well on each label.

Activity: The Magic Mirror

Objective: To raise self-esteem by recognizing positive inner qualities.

• •

We all have positive inner qualities that make us valuable people. Inner qualities are those that we cannot see or touch, but that we carry within us and that other people "see" through our actions. Some positive inner qualities are kindness, generosity, intelligence and a sense of humor.

Pretend The Magic Mirror below can help you see inside yourself. Take a look and discover your own positive inner qualities. Write your qualities on the lines provided, using a different color for each one. Then, using the same colors, fill in the body picture on the next page. How do you show your inner qualities to other people?

Area 4: When People Hurt Us

Activity: Amusement Park

Objective: To understand that the way I treat others can affect the way they treat me.

••

People usually treat you the same way you treat them. If you act friendly, they will be friendly toward you. If you treat others kindly, they are likely to treat you kindly. When you approach someone in a hostile way, they most likely will become defensive and act unfriendly.

In the picture below, the children are acting in many different ways. Put a circle around the children who are doing things that would probably make other people want to treat them nicely. Put an X over the children who are doing things that would probably make other people treat them meanly.

51

Area 4: When People Hurt Us

Activity: Teasing Thermometer

Objective: To differentiate between harmless and malicious teasing.

• •

Everyone gets teased by someone at some time. Harmless teasing can be a friendly way of showing affection, but malicious teasing can be cruel and hurtful.

Look at the pictures below and decide whether the teasing depicted in each picture is friendly or cruel. Show your decision by filling in the mercury level on the thermometer next to each picture. The more friendly the teasing, the lower the mercury level will be. The more cruel the teasing, the higher the mercury level will be.

Activity: Joey's Wagon

Objective: To differentiate between behaviors that are more likely to invite teasing and those that are not.

• •

You may do some things that make it more likely you will be teased. And, there are some things you can do that will make it more likely that you will be left alone.

You are more likely to be teased if you do the following:

- Look scared
- Make funny noises with your body
- Tattle on others
- Get upset easily
- Have poor hygiene
- Do funny things with your body
- Act like a "know-it-all"

You are more likely to be left alone if do the following:

- Don't let harmless teasing bother you
- Don't get upset easily
- Have a sense of humor about yourself
- Mind your own business
- Treat yourself respectfully
- Act confidently
- Have good hygiene

In the picture on the next page, Joey is pulling a wagon full of behaviors he uses all the time. These behaviors encourage other kids to tease him. Help Joey behave in a way that will discourage the teasers. Cut out the behaviors below and glue or tape these new behaviors over the old ones in Joey's wagon. Then change Joey's frown into a smile.

Ignores teasing	**Keeps himself clean**	**Is honest**
Uses a tissue in private	**Minds his own business**	**Makes positive comments**

Picks his nose

Whines

Makes up stories
that aren't true

Tattles

Cries easily

Doesn't brush
his teeth

Activity: Keep Your Cool

Objective: To learn ways to stay calm when being teased.

• •

If you stay cool and calm when someone is teasing you, you will be better able to ignore the teasing and not get upset. When you don't look hot and bothered, the teaser is more likely to stop. It is not always easy to stay cool and calm, but there are things you can do to help yourself.

Julia is trying to stay cool while some kids in her class are teasing her. The list of ideas written in ice blocks on the next page can help her stay calm.   Cut them out and glue or tape them next to and above Julie, forming an ice fort. The ice fort will cool her down and protect her from teasing.

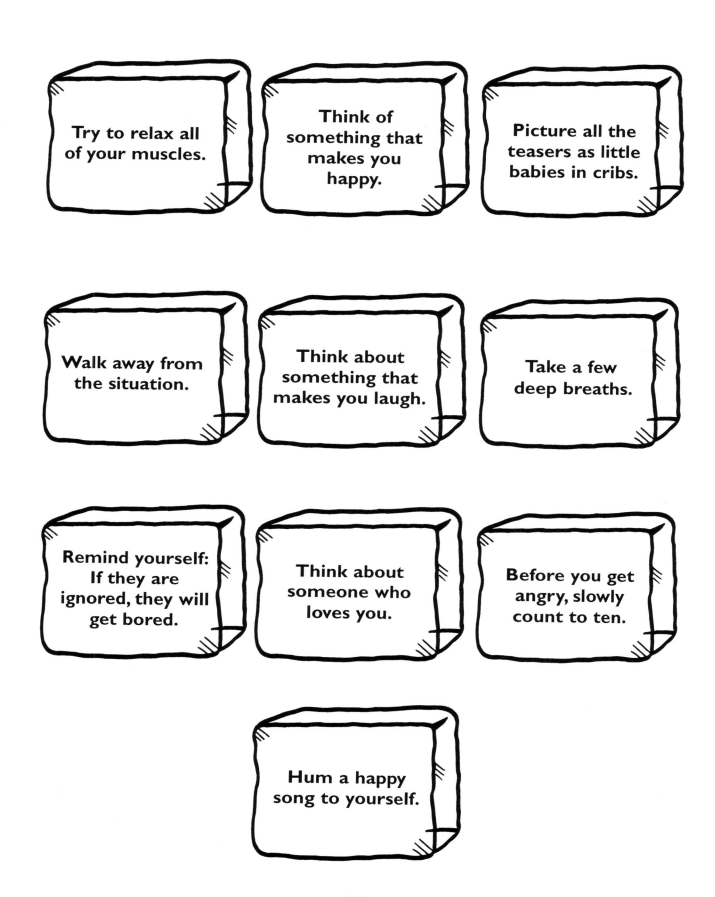

Try to relax all of your muscles.

Think of something that makes you happy.

Picture all the teasers as little babies in cribs.

Walk away from the situation.

Think about something that makes you laugh.

Take a few deep breaths.

Remind yourself: If they are ignored, they will get bored.

Think about someone who loves you.

Before you get angry, slowly count to ten.

Hum a happy song to yourself.

Activity: My Toolbox

Objective: To learn ways to reduce teasing and bullying.

• •

If other children tease or bully you, there are four things you can do that may make them stop.

1. Ignore them. Teasers and bullies need to get a big reaction out of the person they are bothering. If you ignore them, they don't have as much fun and they will look for someone else to pick on, someone who has a bigger reaction.

2. Laugh it off. If the teasing and bullying is more friendly than cruel, you can try to have fun instead of becoming upset. Laughing at yourself is better than feeling bad about yourself. It can also stop the teasers and bullies from bothering you.

3. Avoid them. If you stay away from the teasers and bullies, you make it harder for them to bother you. They will pick on someone else who is closer by.

4. Stick with friends. Teasers and bullies will be more afraid to bother you if you are with people who like and support you. If your friends aren't nearby, stay by a parent, teacher or other adult.

Write one tool phrase (IGNORE THEM, LAUGH IT OFF, AVOID THEM, STICK WITH FRIENDS) in each of the tools below. Color and cut out the tools and the toolbox on the next page. Then glue or tape your tools inside the toolbox and fold the top down. Keep your toolbox in your pocket or your backpack so you are always prepared to encounter teasers and bullies.

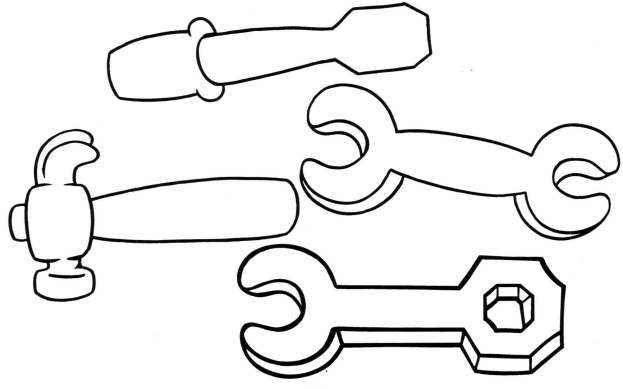

Activity: Using the Tools in My Toolbox

Objective: To understand the benefits of using the tools of ignoring, laughing it off, avoiding, and sticking with friends.

• •

Sometimes we know something in our heads; but, when it comes time to put what we know into practice, we forget to do it. The more we practice new skills, the more likely we are to use them when we need them.

Bobby is being teased. He remembers to use his tools. Read the picture stories and think about what will happen next. Select the ending for each picture story, and place that number in the box next to the picture story.

59

Area 4: When People Hurt Us

Activity: Hurting Inside

Objective: To learn that people may hurt me because they are feeling bad about themselves.

• •

When people hurt us with their teasing or bullying, it is often because they are feeling hurt themselves. When teasers and bullies feel bad about themselves, they may try to get rid of their own pain by making someone else feel bad.

Look at the story sequences below. Number the scenes so that they are in the right order. On the line below the sequence, write what you think the teaser or bully is feeling.

Activity: Calling for Help*

Objective: To understand that when teasing or bullying is severe an adult should be called for help.

• •

*To stress the importance of this text and to ensure the child's safety, this exercise should be completed with adult guidance and discussion.

Talk about this exercise with an adult. Most of the time children can handle teasing and bullying by themselves. But sometimes these behaviors can get out of hand, and then it is important to call an adult for help.

Call an adult in the following situations:

• If you or someone else is crying so hard, you/he can't stop

• If a teaser or bully threatens to hurt you or someone else physically

• If a teaser or bully does hurt you or someone else physically

• If the teaser or bully is an adult

• If any child or adult has a weapon of any kind, even if it is not being used

Look at the following pictures, and talk about them with an adult. Then decide if these children need help from an adult. If it is safe for them to handle the situation by themselves, color the hand next to the picture. If an adult should be called, color the phone next to the picture.

Even healthy relationships encounter problems. What makes a relationship healthy is that, when problems do arise, they are handled efficiently and objectively.

When children learn that certain behaviors cause problems, they can choose to avoid these behaviors. When they understand that both people in a relationship contribute to a problem to some degree, they can learn to take responsibility for their own behavior rather than blaming the other person.

When children are aware of specific problem-solving steps and they know and practice problem-solving techniques, they are better able to manage difficulties.

Activity: The Problem Planet
Objective: To identify behaviors that often cause problems between people.

• •

Because we are all different, it is normal to have problems with each other once in a while. The way we behave toward other people can either help us get along better or cause more problems.

The creatures below live on The Problem Planet. They have a very hard time getting along with each other because of the way they behave. See if you can tell where the creatures on The Problem Planet live by matching their names and the way they behave to their caves. Draw a line from each creature to its cave.

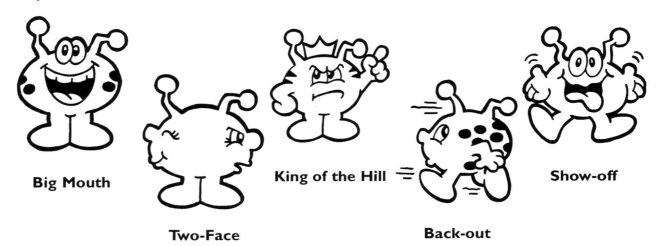

Big Mouth   **King of the Hill**   **Show-off**

Two-Face   **Back-out**

Bossy

Talks behind people's backs

Doesn't keep promises

Can't keep secrets

Conceited

Activity: It Takes Two

Objective: To learn that it takes two people to have an argument.

• •

There are many things in life, such as arguing, that require two people. Some people like to blame others, saying that an argument is all someone else's fault. But no one can have an argument alone. When you are involved in an argument, it is always partly your responsibility.

The pictures below show activities that require two people to accomplish. Draw in the missing half of the picture.

Activity: Problem-Solving Steps

Objective: To learn a formula for problem-solving.

· ·

When there is a problem between you and another person, you can take specific steps to try and solve it. The Five Problem-Solving Steps are as follows:

1. Identify the problem.

2. Brainstorm solutions.

3. Evaluate the solutions.

4. Try one of the solutions.

5. Try another solution if the previous one did not work.

You can practice naming The Five Problem-Solving Steps by helping Jill. Jill wanted to use the steps the next time she had a problem, so she wrote each step on an index card. As she was walking home, a big wind scattered the cards all over the ground. Help Jill by finding each card and numbering it so that she knows the correct order of The Five Problem-Solving Steps.

Activity: The Main Problem

Objective: To practice identifying problems clearly.

· ·

Sometimes it may seem like you have many different problems troubling you at once. When you can look past the smaller problems, you will see the main problem more clearly. This can help you solve the main problem more quickly and easily. And when you solve the main problem, many of the smaller problems are often resolved as well.

To practice identifying the main problem in a situation, look at the picture below. Many problems are depicted, but there is one that is bigger than all the rest. If this main problem were solved, it would solve the smaller problems, too. Draw a circle around the problems, and color the main problem. Write the main problem on the line below.

Area 5: Solving Problems with People

Activity: Brainstorm Bubbles

Objective: To learn how to brainstorm.

Brainstorming is a technique that can help you discover solutions to problems. When you brainstorm, you make a list of *every* possible solution imaginable, without making any judgments about its value. No matter how silly or unrealistic the idea is, add it to your list. The goal is to come up with as many possibilities as you can.

The children below must figure out how to solve the problems that are in front of them. You can help them by brainstorming. Write your ideas in the storm clouds above their heads.

Activity: Tiger Fight

Objective: To consider the consequences prior to choosing a solution.

• •

   Whenever there is more than one possible solution to a problem (and that is almost always), it is important to think about each possibility carefully. Every action you take has a consequence. Thinking about the consequences of each solution, prior to choosing one, will help you decide which would be the best to try first.

   A problem is depicted below. Two tigers are fighting and might hurt each other or someone else. Pretend you are the zookeeper and it is your job to solve this problem. List three possible solutions you could try on the lines provided. Then write what might happen if you tried each one. Finally, choose the solution you think is best and put a star next to it.

Solution 1 _____

Consequence _____

Solution 2 _____

Consequence _____

Solution 3 _____

Consequence _____

Area 5: Solving Problems with People

Activity: Taking Real Steps

Objective: To practice The Five Problem-Solving Steps.

• •

After you learn The Five Problem-Solving Steps, you can practice them by applying them to problem situations you have had in the past. Then the next time you encounter a problem, you will know what to do. The more you practice, the better you will become at solving problems.

On the lines below, list four problems you have had with other people. In the space on the next page, trace the outline of your foot and make four photocopies. Write one of The Five Problem-Solving Steps on each foot. Color all five feet a different color, cut them out, and lay them on the floor in front of you so that you can walk on them. Choose one of the problems on your list and walk through The Five Problem-Solving Steps. As you stand on Step 1, identify your problem; Step 2, brainstorm solutions; Step 3, evaluate solutions; Step 4, try one solution; Step 5, try another solution if the previous one does not work.

_____

_____

_____

_____

_____

_____

Activity: What Would Happen?

Objective: To understand the importance of cooperation.

• •

When two people have a problem in their relationship, it is important they both make an effort to solve the problem. Cooperation requires you work together to find a solution that works for both of you. There is a better chance that a problem will be solved if you practice cooperation.

The people below are in situations where it is important that they cooperate with others. Write what could happen if they did not cooperate.

_____

_____

_____

_____

_____

_____

Activity: Meet Me in the Middle

Objective: To practice identifying ways to compromise.

. . . .

When you compromise with someone, you "meet in the middle." Neither one of you may get exactly what you want; but, if you each give in a little, you will both get something, if not all, you want.

The pictures below show several sets of friends who want to do something together, but they are disagreeing about what to do. As long as the friends disagree, they cannot do anything. Help them meet in the middle by thinking of ways for them to reach a compromise. Write your solutions halfway between both friends.

Area 5: Solving Problems with People

Activity: Sharing and Taking Turns

Objective: To learn that sharing and taking turns makes it easier to get along with others.

• •

When you share and take turns you are being generous, which is the opposite of being selfish. When you are generous, it is easier to get along with other people and to solve any problems you may have with them.

Color the picture below with another person. Divide the crayons or markers in half, with each of you taking a share. Choose one person to start coloring a small area of the picture first. Then the other person takes a turn and colors another small area. Then the first person goes again. Keep sharing the colors and taking turns until the picture is finished.

Area 6: Managing Conflict with People

Relationship conflict is inevitable. However, when conflict management skills are used, there is a better chance that arguments will be handled efficiently and effectively.

When children learn and practice healthy ways to communicate feelings, express anger, and keep conflicts from escalating, they are better equipped to face the quarrels and misunderstandings that are a natural part of most human relationships.

Mastering conflict resolution skills can help an aggressive child act more reasonably and a passive, shy child act more assertively during interactions with others.

Activity: I Feel Statements

Objective: To use "I feel" statements to express problems effectively and keep conflicts from escalating.

••

If you tell someone how you feel in a noncritical way when you are having a conflict, you can keep the conflict from getting bigger. "I feel" statements tell others how you feel when they act in a specific way. When in a conflict situation, state the sentence below and fill in the blanks with your own words:
"When you _____, I feel _____."

The children below are not using "I feel" statements. The way they are talking is creating more angry energy and making their conflict bigger. There are conversation balloons with "I feel" statements on the bottom of the next page. Cut these out and glue or tape them over the original statements.

When you don't share with me, I feel angry.

When you don't understand what I say, I feel frustrated and impatient.

When you call me mean names, I feel hurt.

When we argue all the time, I feel angry and sad.

Area 6: Managing Conflict with People

Activity: Anger Is Okay

Objective: To learn that anger is a normal response to a frustrating situation and to identify ways anger is felt in the body.

· ·

It is normal to feel angry when something you don't like happens. You may feel angry when things do not go your way or when you do not get what you want immediately. Sometimes you may feel angry with another person, even a friend or someone you love. It is normal to feel "angry energy" in your body. The signs of angry energy include tension in your muscles, shortness of breath, rapid heartbeat, and heat on your face.

Circle the situations below that would make you feel angry. Then draw a picture of how you look when you are angry.

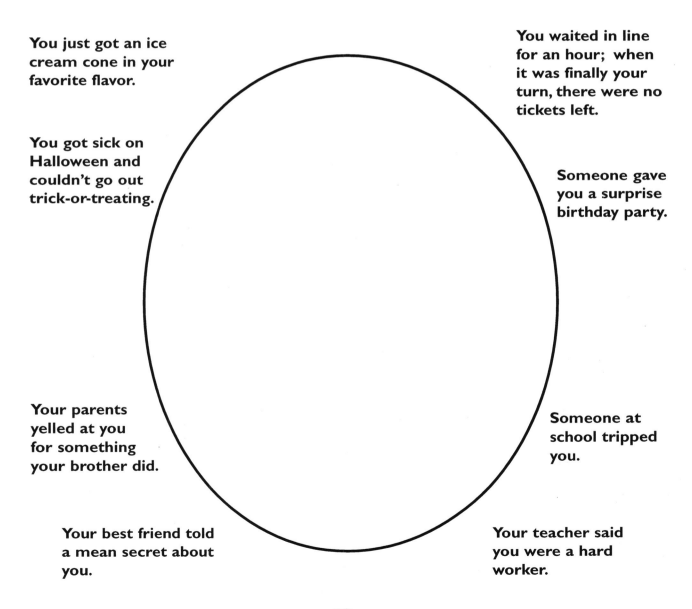

You just got an ice cream cone in your favorite flavor.

You got sick on Halloween and couldn't go out trick-or-treating.

You waited in line for an hour; when it was finally your turn, there were no tickets left.

Someone gave you a surprise birthday party.

Your parents yelled at you for something your brother did.

Someone at school tripped you.

Your best friend told a mean secret about you.

Your teacher said you were a hard worker.

Area 6: Managing Conflict with People

Activity: Angry Andy and Angry Al

Objective: To learn safe ways to express anger.

• •

It is always okay to feel angry and to let out your angry energy. But it is not okay to let it out in a way that could hurt someone or something. It is important to find safe ways to let out your angry energy.

Angry Andy and Angry Al are angry with each other. They need to find ways to express their anger safely. Look at the pictures around Andy and Al. Circle the pictures that show safe ways to let out anger. Put an X over the pictures that show ways that could hurt someone or something.

Activity: Deep Breathing

Objective: To learn that a calm state helps people manage conflict and to practice deep breathing to calm down.

. . . .

You can manage conflict better when you are feeling calm. But sometimes it is hard to calm down if you are angry or upset. Taking slow, deep breaths is one way to calm yourself. When you breathe slowly and deeply, your body releases tension and you feel more peaceful.

Color and cut out each of the circled numbers below. Tape the numbers onto a table in front of you, putting #1 closest to you and #5 farthest away from you. Color and cut out the "breather ball." Place the breather ball on the table directly in front of you. Inhale deeply through the nose and exhale through the mouth onto the breather ball. See how far you can get the breather ball to move. If it moves as far as #1, you score one point; if it moves as far as #2, you score two points; and so on. See how many points you can score with five deep breaths. Then try to beat your record.

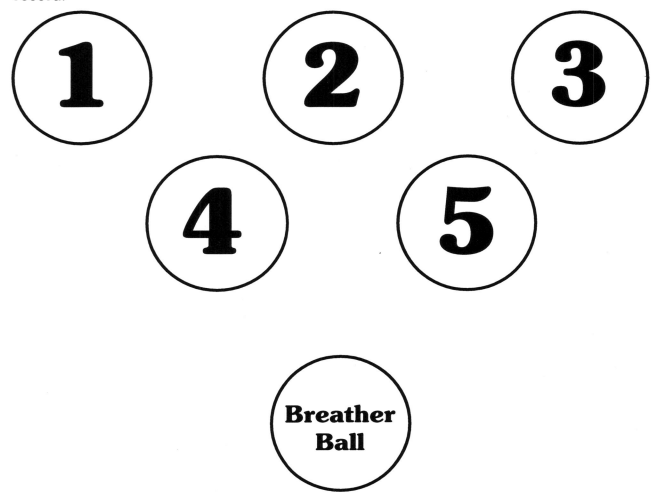

Activity: **Put the Problem Outside Yourself**

Objective: **To** see **conflict as a separate entity.**

. . . .

If you blame someone else for a conflict, or if they blame you, it only makes you both angrier and the conflict escalates. If you see the conflict as neither person's fault, as something outside both of you, you can stay calm and will more likely be able to solve the conflict.

Brianna and Bryan are blaming each other for three different situations. This will make them angrier, and their conflict will become bigger. Help them to see the problem as something outside themselves. Without blaming either of them, write the problems in the boxes between them.

Activity: Good Time, Bad Time

Objective: To identify the best and worst times to resolve a conflict.

. . . .

Some times are better than others to resolve a conflict. You will have better results if both you and the other person are calm and relaxed and if there is enough time to sit down and talk peacefully.

Copy this page and lay it flat on a table. Lay a pencil in the middle of the clock below. Spin the pencil. When it stops, read the description that the pencil is pointing to. Decide if this would be a good or a bad time to resolve a conflict.

Activity: The Wall of Conflict

Objective: To focus on one problem at a time to keep a conflict from escalating.

Focusing on one problem at a time can help you resolve a conflict more easily. Even if there are many things you are angry about, you will stay calmer and keep your conflict from getting bigger if you work on only one problem at a time.

Joe and Jenny are having an argument about who should get to choose the television program they will watch. This is a small problem that makes a small wall of conflict between them. But Joe and Jenny are also bringing up other problems at the same time. This makes the wall of conflict between them bigger. Color and cut out all the problems on the next page that Joe and Jenny are bringing up. Glue or tape these problems on top of the original problem. Watch the wall of conflict get bigger as more problems are added.

Who should pick the television program?

You always tattle
on me.

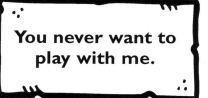

You never want to
play with me.

You borrowed my
favorite T-shirt and
never gave it back.

You never share
your candy.

You never pass the
ball to me in
soccer.

You always make
fun of me.

You don't let me
play ball with you.

You cheat when we
play cards.

You act like a baby.

Activity: Past and Present

Objective: To focus on the present situation to keep a conflict from escalating.

• •

When you are having a conflict, bringing up past situations will only add more angry energy and make the conflict bigger. Keeping your conversation limited to the present situation will keep the conflict more manageable.

The following statements could arise when two people are having a conflict. Some of the statements are about the past, which will make the conflict bigger. Some of the statements focus only on the present, which will keep the conflict manageable. If the statement is about the past, color the time machine with a dark color to block out the message. If the statement is about the present, color the time machine with a light color to keep the message visible.

You're not sharing the jelly beans.

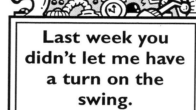
Last week you didn't let me have a turn on the swing.

Last summer you scratched up my bike.

The last two times we colored, you didn't share the crayons.

Every time I see you, you say something rude to me.

You just spilled your soda on my new dress.

You're not letting me have a turn at shooting baskets.

What you just said hurt my feelings.

Activity: A Letter of Apology

Objective: To learn the importance of apologizing and to practice apologizing.

• •

When you have hurt someone or done something that helped cause a conflict, it is important to apologize for your words or actions. Apologizing means saying "I'm sorry" for what you have done. Saying "I'm sorry" is respectful and polite. It tells another person that you regret what you said or did and that your relationship is important.

Think of something you have done recently that hurt another person. In the space below, write a letter of apology. Cut out the letter and give it to the person you have hurt.

Dear

From

Activity: Dear Diary

Objective: To understand the importance of forgiveness and to practice forgiveness.

••

When others hurt you, you can forgive them. When you forgive, you release the bad feelings you have inside and you can start over fresh in your relationship. If you have been hurt badly, it may be hard to forgive someone right away, but usually over time it can be done.

In the diary below, write the names of two people who have hurt you. Draw a picture of yourself under the conversation balloon. Write what you forgive each person for in the conversation balloon. At the bottom of the page, write something for which you would like them to forgive you. Plan a time when you can tell them you forgive them in person.